LUDWIG VAN BEETHOVEN (about 1823)
Engraving after a drawing by Martin Tejcek

BEETHOVEN

ELEVEN BAGATELLES OPUS 119
FOR THE PIANO

EDITED BY WILLARD A. PALMER

THEMATIC INDEX

Alfred
Second Edition
Copyright © MMV by Alfred Publishing Co., Inc.
All rights reserved.   Printed in USA.

Cover art: A detail from Meadows before Greifswald
by Casper David Friedrich (1774–1840)
Oil on canvas, ca. 1820
Kunsthalle, Hamburg
Archiv für Kunst und Geschichte, Berlin

Opus 119, No. 4. Autograph of the first page.
Courtesy of the Staatsbibliothek (Preussischer Kulturbesitz),
Musikabteilung, Berlin.

BEETHOVEN

Ludwig van Beethoven was born at Bonn, Germany, on December 16, 1770. He died March 26, 1827, in Vienna. Like most of the great masters, he was a child prodigy and he held several important musical positions at the age of 12. At this time his teacher was Christian Gottlob Neefe, a well-educated musician of high repute. From Neefe he studied harmony and theory and became acquainted with J. S. Bach's keyboard music as well as the works of Handel and many of the Italian and French masters. He also became proficient as a violinist and violist. Beethoven was later to study very briefly with Mozart and for a longer period with Haydn, Albrechtsberger and Salieri. But it was to Neefe that he felt the most keenly indebted for his musical background. When he was 22 years old he wrote to Neefe, "Should I ever become a great man, you will have had a share in it."

Beethoven's initial impact on the musical world was as a brilliant virtuoso of the piano. Those who heard him wrote that his playing was unlike anything ever heard before. His contemporaries were astonished at his "daring deviations from one motive to another," his "elemental force" and his "titanic execution." At this time he had composed many works but had not gained much recognition as a creative artist, except for the fact that the musical world of Vienna was amazed at his ability to improvise on any theme presented to him. Because of this ability, he became extremely popular as a performer for the Viennese aristocracy.

Beethoven's growing deafness caused him to eventually withdraw from public life and to devote all of his time to composing. One can trace the growth of his marvelous genius as his heroic struggles with his own infirmities were reflected in his works. His progress as a creative artist was continuous throughout his lifetime, and as he progressed the art of music also progressed. He transformed even such obvious forms as the *theme and variations* into triumphs of musical architecture, and his contribution to the larger forms, such as the *sonata, concerto* and *symphony*, were so profound that they would require volumes for adequate discussion.

ORIGIN

The eleven *Bagatelles,* Opus 119, were composed over a period of several months, during the latter part of 1822 and the beginning of 1823. They were first published as a complete collection by Clementi & Co. of London in 1823. The last five of these pieces had been included, several years earlier, in the third part of Friedrich Stark's *Wiener Pianoforte Schule.* The *Bagatelles* were published later in 1823 in Paris by Maurice Schlesinger and in 1824 by Sauer and Leidesdorf of Vienna.

In his book, *The Authentic English Editions of Beethoven* (Faber & Faber, London, 1963), Alan Tyson convincingly states that the Clementi edition is the first and only authentic edition of Op. 119, and that the Schlesinger edition is merely a reprint of the Clementi edition and not a very accurate one. It contains many obvious errors that did not seem important enough to enumerate in our footnotes. The Viennese edition seems to have little textual value, since it is obviously a reprint of the Schlesinger edition, with several additional typographical errors.

This collection of *Bagatelles* is mentioned in no fewer than 16 of Beethoven's letters, most of which were addressed to C. F. Peters, to whom the work was first offered. Peters refused to accept the *Bagatelles.* He wrote Beethoven a letter saying, "You should consider it beneath your dignity to waste your time on such trifles, which anyone could have written." Beethoven's reply was that Peters had "no artistic judgment." He added that Peters was only thinking that he might have received a major work for the same fee. It is obvious from Beethoven's letters that he valued these "trifles" highly and that he enjoyed writing them. In his own assessment of these works, Beethoven's judgment was correct, and it is fortunate that he took the time to write music that is easy enough to serve as such excellent material for the young student.

In a letter to his pupil, Ferdinand Ries, in 1823, Beethoven wrote that "the first six Bagatelles and the last five belong together, in two parts." Thus, the pieces may be performed not only as individual selections, but as two separate suites.

The present edition was prepared from the following sources:

1. Facsimiles of the autographs (1822-23):
   a. Nos. 1-6, courtesy of the Staatsbibliothek (Preussischer Kulturbesitz), Musikabteilung, Berlin.
   b. No. 8 and the first part of No. 9, courtesy of the Beethovenhaus, Bonn.
   c. Nos. 10 & 11 and the second part of No. 9, courtesy of the Bibliotheque Nationale, Paris.
   (The location of the autograph of No. 7 is not known.)

2. A facsimile of the first English edition (Clementi & Co., London, 1823), courtesy of the British Museum, London.

3. A facsimile of the 2nd printing of the first English edition (Clementi & Co., London, 1824), courtesy of the British Museum, London.

4. A facsimile of the first French edition (Maurice Schlesinger, Paris, 1823), courtesy of the Library of Congress, Washington, D.C.

Beethoven's original text is presented in dark print, and all editorial suggestions appear in light print, with explanations in footnotes. In a number of cases, dynamic indications, slurs, etc., are present in both of the earliest editions but missing in the autograph. In such cases, they are presumed to be corrections made by Beethoven and are added to our text without special comment.

BEETHOVEN'S LEGATO

According to Czerny, who was Beethoven's pupil, Beethoven's legato was "controlled to an incomparable degree, which at that time all pianists regarded as impossible of execution, for even after Mozart's time the choppy, short, detached manner of playing was the fashion." "Beethoven himself told me," Czerny added, "that he had heard Mozart play on various occasions and that Mozart had accustomed himself to the manner of playing on the harpsichord, then more frequently used, a style in no way adapted to the pianoforte, which was still in its infancy." Beethoven is said to have looked with disdain upon the old Mozart style of playing, which he called "finger dancing" and "manual air-sawing." This may be shocking news to those who have read so much in praise of Mozart's legato, which Mozart himself described as "flowing like oil."

The importance of Beethoven's attitude toward legato playing is emphasized by the fact that he admired Clementi's playing more than Mozart's. He endorsed Clementi's piano method from the moment it became available (around 1803). In this method, Clementi states, "When the composer leaves the LEGATO, and the STACCATO to the performer's taste; the best rule is, to adhere chiefly to the LEGATO; reserving the STACCATO to give SPIRIT occasionally to certain passages, and set off the HIGHER BEAUTIES of the LEGATO." (Capital letters and punctuation are Clementi's.) Such instructions are applicable to the performance of Beethoven's music. Beethoven marked some of his measures with meticulous care and was merciless in his condemnation of any copyist who ignored such markings, or any publisher who printed them incorrectly. On one occasion he insisted that the publisher retrieve all the copies that had been sold to make corrections in them. But many measures were left without indications of staccato, legato, phrasing or dynamics.

BEETHOVEN'S USE OF STACCATO

Clementi's instructions for the performance of staccato may be applied to Beethoven's music. The following is quoted from Clementi's *INTRODUCTION TO THE ART OF PLAYING ON THE PIANOFORTE.* (Capitalization and punctuation are Clementi's.)

> The best general rule, is to keep down the keys of the instrument the full LENGTH of every note; for when the contrary is required, the notes are marked either thus:

called in ITALIAN, STACCATO; denoting DISTINCTNESS, and SHORTNESS of sound; which is produced by lifting the finger up, as soon as it has struck the key: or they are marked thus

which when composers are EXACT in their writing, means LESS staccato than the preceding mark; the finger, therefore, is kept down somewhat longer: or thus

which means STILL LESS staccato: the nice degrees of MORE and LESS, however, depend on the CHARACTER, and PASSION of the piece; the STYLE of which must be WELL OBSERVED by the performer.

It is worth noting that while C.P.E. Bach considered the staccato wedge and the dot identical in meaning, Beethoven definitely did not. In a letter to his friend, Karl Holz, August, 1825, he wrote " 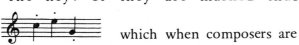 are not identical."

BEETHOVEN'S USE OF THE SLUR

Beethoven, like Bach, Haydn and the great instrumental composers, used slurs as if they were bowing indications for stringed instruments. When a violinist changes the direction of his bow after only a few notes are played, it is usually for the purpose of effect.

The change of bow direction may be used to give a slight emphasis to the first note played in the new direction, as the bow "digs" slightly into the string. The wind instrumentalist produces a similar effect by "tonguing."

If a violinist were to play the opening phrase of the first *Bagatelle* (page 10):

it would be bowed as follows: ⊓ = down bow; V up bow

The effect of exaggerated separation between the slurred notes and the note following the slur is NOT intended:

The purpose of such bowing is to produce a slight stress or emphasis on the first beat of the first full measure. This might be indicated by the following notation:

In the 28th and 29th measures of the first *Bagatelle* (page 11), Beethoven indicates the following phrasing:

The following "pianistic" treatment constitutes an undesirable, exaggerated effect:

The breaks between slurs should be almost imperceptible. The short slurs are used mainly to indicate slight emphasis on the first note of each pair:

When Beethoven wanted a short note at the end of a slur he was usually careful to indicate it, as he did in the sixth *Bagatelle*, beginning with the 7th measure (page 22):

In *cantabile* passages such as that in the 11th *Bagatelle,* beginning with the 11th measure (page 31), the function of the slur in Beethoven's music is particularly important. Beethoven certainly intended no break at all between the slurs, which serve to indicate that he did want the first note of each group of slurred notes to receive a certain emphasis:

written:

played:

MUSIC WITHOUT SLURS

In music for stringed instruments, when no slurs are marked, each note calls for a change in the direction of the bow. The change can be made by a skillful player with practically no break in the continuity of the tone, but the resulting articulation is different than a series of notes played with no change in direction of the bow.

Some of Beethoven's "unmarked measures" might best be left unmarked for this reason. The performer should keep this in mind when playing passages marked with slurs in light print (editorial slurs), as in the opening measures of the 2nd *Bagatelle* (page 14):

The absence of slurs does not necessarily eliminate legato, but places a certain importance on the individual notes. The fact that this same piece contains a number of notes marked staccato is helpful in verifying our conviction that these notes, which are unmarked, should be played legato, as the Clementi method recommends. See the 2nd paragraph under BEETHOVEN'S LEGATO, on page 4.

In his book, *BEETHOVEN,* Sir Donald Francis Tovey expressed the opinion that, where Beethoven has not made up his own mind, he has not invited editors of his music to make it up for him. Who, then, must decide how such a passage is to be played? As Clementi emphasizes, it is left to the performer's taste. Good music deserves to be interpreted, and the performer should have a share in the creation of it, but such a privilege is only allowable in the light of adequate knowledge of the composer's style and traditions.

In Beethoven's music, many measures are not marked because they are obviously played like similar measures previously marked. In the 1st *Bagatelle,* (page 10), for example, the opening phrase is clearly marked, and we may be certain that the following similar phrase is to be played the same way; but the articulation of the notes in measures 5, 6 and 7 are left to the discretion of the individual. With such considerations in mind, it will be obvious which of the editorial indications should be considered to be suggestions (one person's opinion of how the music might be acceptably interpreted). On some occasions, these suggestions may save the teacher a bit of time and trouble, and on others they may serve as points of departure.

BEETHOVEN'S ORNAMENTS

In determining the proper execution of Beethoven's ornaments, a few pertinent facts must be considered. As a student, Beethoven was taught to play ornaments in the manner prescribed by C.P.E. Bach. As a teacher he used C.P.E. Bach's *ESSAY ON THE TRUE ART OF PLAYING KEYBOARD INSTRUMENTS* and Clementi's *ART OF PLAYING ON THE PIANOFORTE.* C.P.E. Bach insisted, as did other 18th-century theorists, that all trills must begin on the upper note. Clementi stressed that they generally begin on the upper note but allowed an occasional departure from the rule to preserve a legato with the preceding note. Beethoven was quite aware of the problems that might be created by the allowance of such exceptions and, in passages where there might be confusion, he often inserted a small note indicating the starting note of the trill. In the absence of such a note or fingering indicating a principal-note start, we may be reasonably sure that the trill begins on the upper note.

Many music editors insist that, since Beethoven lived in the 19th century, his trills must begin on the principal note. They lose sight of the fact that the trill from the principal note did not begin to come into general use until the publication of Johann Nepomuk Hummel's *COMPLETE THEORETICAL AND PRACTICAL COURSE* in 1828, a year after Beethoven's death.

After Hummel's book was published, many famous artists, including Czerny, who was a great admirer of Hummel, influenced others by playing Beethoven's trills incorrectly. This was not because Beethoven had allowed him to play them in such a fashion. Czerny himself relates that, when he played the *Sonata Pathetique* for Beethoven, the master agreed to take him as a pupil with the proviso that he obtain a copy of C.P.E. Bach's *ESSAY* and bring it with him to the first lesson. We may be certain that Beethoven wanted to point out to Czerny that the trills in this sonata must be played beginning on the upper note.

Only the ornaments used in this book are discussed here.

1. THE SHORT APPOGGIATURA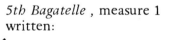

All appoggiaturas are played *on the beat.* This is in accordance with the rules of C.P.E. Bach, Clementi and even Hummel.

The only appoggiaturas in Beethoven's Opus 119 appear in the fifth *Bagatelle* (page 20). In this selection the single appoggiaturas are written as small 32nd notes.

In C.P.E. Bach's *ESSAY*, he endorsed the notation of all appoggiaturas in their real values and regarded such notation as indispensable, particularly in indicating the precise values of long appoggiaturas. As for the short appoggiatura, he recognized the fact that an accurate representation of the time consumed was not practical. In his *ESSAY* he says that they "carry one, two, three or more tails and are played so rapidly that the following note loses scarcely any of its length.

5th Bagatelle , measure 1
written:

played, approximately:

2. THE DOUBLE APPOGGIATURA

The double appoggiatura is also played *on the beat.* The fifth *Bagatelle* contains double appoggiaturas in measures 10, 12 and 22. They all appear as pairs of small sixteenth notes in both first editions. In the autograph, one pair is written as small 32nds. The values are of no consequence, since they are to be played as rapidly as possible.

This particular configuration of the double appoggiatura (two small notes ascending diatonically to the main note) is also called a *schleifer* or *slide.* This type of schleifer was invariably played rapidly and *on the beat.*

5th Bagatelle, measure 10
written:

played:

3. THE TRILL *tr*

All trills begin on the *upper note* unless the *composer* gives some indication to the contrary.

The small notes after the trilled note are used to end the trill and are called the "suffix." These notes become part of the trill and are played with the same speed as the other notes of the trill.

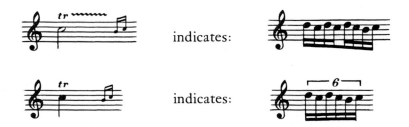

indicates:

The number of repercussions depends upon the tempo of the composition and the skill and taste of the player. Trills of reasonably long duration are usually played with a suffix, whether the small notes are indicated or not.

All of the trills in Opus 119 begin on the *upper note* except those in the seventh *Bagatelle* (page 26). In this selection Beethoven carefully indicated a departure from the normal procedure by giving a choice of 4 5 or 3 4 for playing the trill. Beethoven provides fingering indications for none of the other trills in the entire volume. We may be certain that the trills in the other *Bagatelles* in this series should be played in the *normal* way, beginning on the *upper note*.

4. THE TURN ∾

The symbol for the turn may be used as follows:

   a. The accented turn

   In this case, the turn is played *on the beat*.

indicates: or or

   b. The unaccented turn

   In this case, the turn is played *after the beat*.

indicates: or

indicates: or

Beethoven occasionally used small notes to indicate the turn. These notes may sometimes be considered a realization of a turn over a note, and sometimes an unaccented turn between two notes.

indicates: or

BEETHOVEN'S PEDALING

Beethoven is known to have made lavish use of the pedal. Czerny remarked that he used it "far more than he indicated it in his works." The light Viennese piano used by Beethoven during his years of concertizing did not sustain tones as long as the modern piano. For this reason, Beethoven's pedal markings (or the lack of them) cannot serve as much of a guide as to how to play his music on our present instruments. Once again, we are left to our own decisions.

In his autographs, Beethoven used a small circle to indicate the release of the pedal. In printed editions, the indications *Ped.* * have been generally used. In this book we use the more modern indication⌐_____⌐which more precisely indicates where the pedal is to be depressed and released.

BEETHOVEN'S RUBATO

Although many modern pianists have expressed abhorrence at the use of rubato in Beethoven's music, one can be sure that Beethoven used it. Schindler says, "He adopted tempo rubato in the proper sense of the term, as the subject and situation might demand, without the slightest caricature." He also remarked, "Beethoven changed the tempo as the feelings changed."

It seems, from the reports of his contemporaries, that Beethoven did not allow his pupils as much license as he permitted himself. To him it was important that the time be counted correctly, and he admonished many players to "play the music as I wrote it." But this does not mean that he did not permit freedom of *interpretation.* Upon hearing Marie Bigot de Morogues play one of his sonatas, he said to her, "That is not exactly the reading I should have given, but go ahead. If it is not exactly myself, it is something better."

RECOMMENDED READING

Bach, Carl Philipp Emanuel. ESSAY ON THE TRUE ART OF PLAYING KEYBOARD INSTRUMENTS, W. W. Norton & Co., New York, 1949.

BEETHOVEN: IMPRESSIONS OF CONTEMPORARIES, G. Schirmer, Inc., New York, 1926.

Donington, Robert. THE INTERPRETATION OF EARLY MUSIC, Faber & Faber, 24 Russel Square, London, 1967.

Dorian, Frederick. THE HISTORY OF MUSIC IN PERFORMANCE, W. W. Norton & Co., New York, 1942.

Schonberg, Harold C. THE GREAT PIANISTS FROM MOZART TO THE PRESENT, Simon and Schuster, New York, 1963.

Tovey, Sir Donald Francis. BEETHOVEN, Oxford University Press, London, 1945.

Tyson, Alan. THE AUTHENTIC EDITIONS OF BEETHOVEN, Faber & Faber, London, 1963.

ACKNOWLEDGEMENTS

I would like to express my thanks to Morton Manus and Irving Chasnov for the meticulous care with which they helped to prepare the edition; and to Judith Simon Linder for invaluable assistance in the research necessary for the realization of this edition and for her help in preparing the manuscript.

1. BAGATELLE IN G MINOR

Allegretto

(a) Most editions have the following phrasing:

This is, of course, not indicated by Beethoven, and the performer must decide which phrasing he prefers.

(b) The turn is given as shown in the autograph. In both of the first editions it stands between the A and C and could be realized:

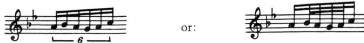

or:

(c) The wedge-shaped staccato marks, differing from the ordinary dots used in the opening measure, are found in both of the first editions and in the autograph. See the discussion, BEETHOVEN'S USE OF STACCATO, page 4.

ⓓ The text here is given according to the autograph and the Clementi edition. The Schlesinger edition has:

12

ⓔ The wedge-shaped staccato marks are found in both of the first editions but are missing in the autograph.

(f) Most editions show all notes staccato in measures 55 through 65. The slurs in light print emphasize the shift of rhythm so characteristic of Beethoven's style. No perceptible break should be made between the slurs, but a slight emphasis should be given the first note of each group of four.

(g) Our text here is according to the first edition and the Schlesinger edition. The autograph has a quarter rest on the first count of the measure and the G on the second.

(h) The arpeggiations appear in the first edition and in the Schlesinger edition, but not in the autograph. They were undoubtedly added by Beethoven.

2. BAGATELLE IN C MAJOR

Andante con moto

ⓐ   All pedaling in this selection is optional. Beethoven gave no pedal indications.

ⓑ Both the first edition and the Schlesinger edition show the final note as it appears above.

The autograph, however, has

3. BAGATELLE IN D MAJOR

(a) Most editions have [music example]. None of this phrasing was indicated by Beethoven. He probably

wanted a legato, but with each note played clearly and distinctly. See the discussion MUSIC WITHOUT SLURS, page 6.

Da capo fin' al segno 𝄋
ed allora la Coda

(b) The lowest note in this chord is scratched out in the autograph but appears in the first edition and the Schlesinger edition.

(c) Beethoven's Italian is translated literally as follows: "From the beginning, ending at the sign 𝄋, and then the Coda." On *D.C.*, do not take the repeats indicated in measures 8 and 16.

18

Coda

ⓓ The lowest note of the chord is missing in the autograph but appears in the first edition and in the Schlesinger edition.

4. BAGATELLE IN A MAJOR

Andante cantabile

Compare with the first page of the autograph, reproduced on page 2.

(a) The number of notes encompassed by the slurs differs in the autograph and in the first edition. Some slurs present in the first edition are not found in the authograph.

(b) The natural signs, missing in the autograph here and in measures 6 and 14, were added in the second printing of the first edition.

(c) The trill is missing in the Schlesinger edition, undoubtedly an oversight, since it is present in the autograph and in the first edition.

(d) The ♯ before the D appears in the autograph, but is missing in the first edition and the Schlesinger edition.

20

5. BAGATELLE IN C MINOR

Risoluto

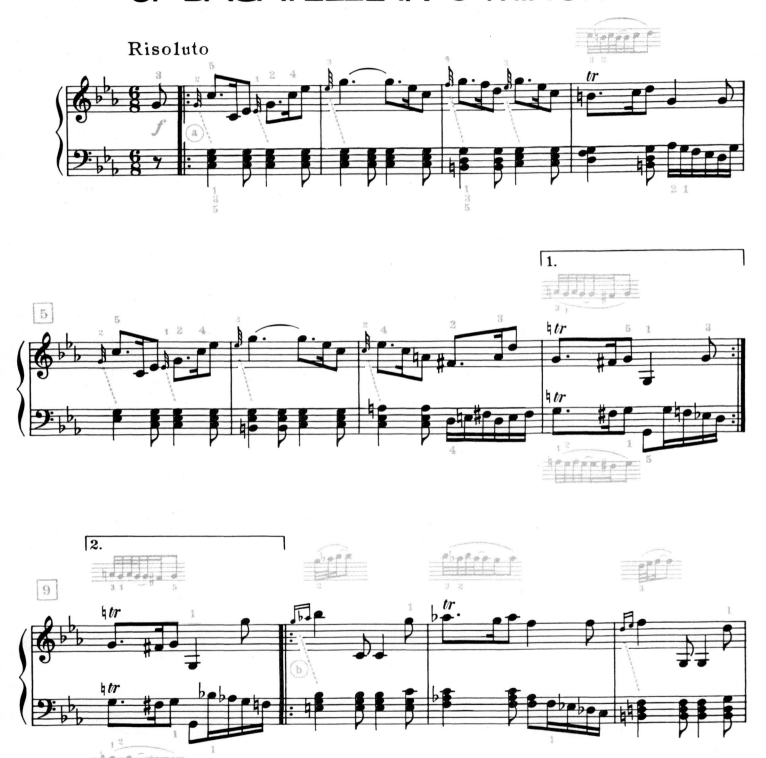

(a) The appoggiaturas should be played as rapidly as possible, and *on the beat*. See the discussion THE SHORT APPOGGIATURA, page 7.

(b) See the discussion THE DOUBLE APPOGGIATURA, page 7.

6. BAGATELLE IN G MAJOR

Andante

Allegretto leggiermente

(a)   The *p* is from the first edition.

(b)   Here the autograph adds *leichtlich vorgetragen* (lightly executed), a translation of the Italian *leggiermente*.

(c) Here the autograph has

Since the first edition and the Schlesinger edition both have the tied D ♮ , we assume this correction was made by Beethoven.

l'istesso tempo

(d) The autograph has *Dieselbe Bewegung* (the same tempo), a German translation of *l'istesso tempo.*

(e) The original sources have B, probably an error.

(f)   This trill appears in the autograph but is missing in both of the earliest editions.

7. BAGATELLE IN C MAJOR

Allegro, ma non troppo

ⓐ The Schlesinger edition gives the trill fingering "3 4 or 4 5." In the first (English) edition the system of + 1 2 3 4 was used, with the + indicating the thumb, so the numbers "2 3 or 3 4" found in that edition are the equivalent of the "3 4 or 4 5" in the Schlesinger edition. This fingering indicates that the trill begins on the principal note. We assume that the remaining trills in the selection also begin on the principal note, but the performer may decide this for himself. See the discussion THE TRILL, page 8.

ⓑ The trill may begin slowly, gradually increasing in the number of repercussions per measure as it continues.

8. BAGATELLE IN C MAJOR

Moderato cantabile

ⓐ In the autograph, the lower voice for the first two counts of the measure is a half note, D (natural). Because this measure appears as shown above (D, D♯) in the first edition as well as the Schlesinger edition, we assume the correction was made by Beethoven.

9. BAGATELLE IN A MINOR

ⓐ **Vivace moderato**

ⓐ The tempo is given according to both first editions. The autograph has *Vivace assai ed un poco sentimentale.*

10. BAGATELLE IN A MAJOR

Allegramente

ⓐ Not  as in some editions.

11. BAGATELLE IN B♭ MAJOR

Andante, ma non troppo

(a)   The first editions have **C**. The autograph has **¢**

(b)   The ♮ before the E is missing in the first editions and in the *Schlesinger* edition.